Thriftology 102: Blazers, Suits & Sport Coats

Make Money Flipping Balzers, Sports Coats & Suits At Thrift Store Prices For Retail Profits

Introduction

The online reselling business is a booming industry and with the economy today, it is a welcome source of additional income. Although there is a variety of merchandise to resell, blazers, coats and suits are proving to be one the most lucrative. These items offer some of the best advantages in the reselling business.

They are highly in demand, being fashion staples. They are carried by a majority of thrift stores, making them easy to source. They are easy to store, to list and to ship making them perfect merchandise for beginner and expert business owners alike. The supply, demand and logistics are already in place and all that is needed is your participation in this industry!

This guide will present you with step by step information on how to start, source, run, manage and ultimately grow and expand your reselling business. The steps in this book are:

Step One: Discover fashion thrifting and reselling
Step Two: Understand your merchandise
Step Three: Open your shop
Step Four: Cross and up sell
Step Five: Build a network

Some of the topics and highlights of this guide are:

Thrifting tips
5 Reasons why I love selling blazers, coats and suits
Anatomy and measuring blazers, coats and suits
50 profitable brands
eBay and Etsy
Choosing a business to price and sell your items
6 Profitable selling points
How to take fantastic pictures
How to take amazing listings

Most cost effective shipping method

Table of Contents

Step One: Discover Thrifting

Types & Differences of Thrift Stores

Clothing thrift stores or thrift stores in general are your main supply source for your merchandise. They are the indispensable partner in your business, which means it is important to know as much as you can about these businesses so you can maximize your thrifting runs. While there are other sources for your merchandise, thrift stores are your priority since this is where you can find the best deals for your business.

There are three different kinds of thrift stores:

Chain
Independent
Specialty

Chain thrift stores are owned and run by big companies. They are located in prime locations in town and offer a wide variety of merchandise aside from clothes. Goodwill and Salvation Army outlets are some examples. When chain thrift stores are located in upscale neighborhoods, you may be able to find high quality items in their inventory. Expect high traffic in these stores which means more competition for you.

Independent stores are owned by individuals or small group. While these stores may not have the same quantity of merchandise as with the chain stores, you can get a better access with proprietors and negotiate directly with them. These stores are usually located outside prime locations and may not be as well advertised as the bigger stores. Finding them may be a challenge but when you do will prove to be very rewarding.

When you do find thrift stores that specialize on clothing, make sure to build a relationship with them. These stores will most probably carry more than enough to fill your inventory with blazers, coats and suits. They know their merchandise well and will usually only carry items that are in a condition good enough for you to resell them for a profit.

There are other thrift store types out there, like vintage or consignment. They may have the items that you need for your inventory. Remember, thrifting is not a science; luck may have more to do with finding that great deal on a branded blazer, coat or suit. However, knowing and expanding your thrift store network will definitely increase your chances in striking gold.

Aside from thrift stores, there are other venues that can supply you with a steady stream of merchandise for you to resell. While some of these other options may not match the same deal that you can get with thrift stores, they may have items that can still net you with a profit.

Some of these stores are:

Clothing outlets or discount stores- these are known to have great deals, sometimes offering you up to 75% discount of the original price. These are in brand new condition and with tags still intact. As you may know, tags can add value when you resell items.

Garage sales- you need to be in the lookout for these kinds of sales on classified ads or on local community boards. Clothes are staples in garage sales and you may find more than one blazer, coat or suit on one site alone. If you are thinking that only middle-class neighborhood will have these sales, then think again. The more affluent areas in town may have garage sales for spring cleaning, charity or just for the fun of it, these are the best places to find high-end items that you may never get elsewhere.

Estate sales- these events happen when someone has died or someone is moving and excess items needed to be monetized instead of transported. Expect vintage and high quality blazers, coats and suits to be sold here. Make sure to be prepared for this kind of sales as they will be highly publicized. Sales will most probably take an auction format or bulk sale, especially for clothing items.

Flea markets- while these kinds of stores may not have the higher quality items that you are looking for; it is still worthwhile to go because of their competitive prices. Be there as early as you can and have a quick look at all the items being sold by all clothing sellers. Then make quick decisions before you lose the opportunity. Be wary though; keep your eye out for any damage that may be beyond repair.

Here are some links that can help you find a thrift store near you:

1. Thrift store directory
2. Thrift store listing
3. Thrift shop finder
4. Sample Google map search for thrift stores
5. Online thrift store directory

In-store Thrifting Tips

Bargaining and negotiating skills are your most important skills when thrifting. Everything in the store will not have a fixed price, even if the personnel say they are. Most personnel are under instructions not to negotiate but if you can contact the business owner, he will be in the position to make a deal with you.

Also be mindful of the purchase price. Never settle for any price even if it is already low by your standards. Your profit margin relies primarily on your purchase price, the lower you can buy it the higher profit could be at the end of your business month.

Go out of your way to befriend the owners or personnel. They may be able to give you inside information on the next shipment of items that will give you first pick of the lot. Also, be sure to mark your calendars with any promo, sales or discount events that the store will regularly have.

Stay focused when you do your thrift runs. Thrift stores have a wide range of merchandise in them, both clothing and non-clothing. It is easy to get sidetracked when you see something that you can personally use. Stick to your budget and buy only to stock your inventory. Be mindful of resources other than money, such as time and effort. Give yourself just enough time for every store on your thrifting run so you can cover as wide an area as possible.

5 Reasons Why I Love Selling Blazers, Coats & Suits

I have been in the online buying and selling business for several years now and until now blazers, coats and suits are still my favorite merchandise to sell. Here are my reasons; maybe they could be yours too:

1. They are fast moving. These clothing items are always in demand because of their function and fashion. This means there is always a market for these items. On the other hand, if I have a blazer that is currently not in season, I can just store it away without any special storage considerations. When the time is right, I can just take it out of storage and it will still be in the same condition.
2. They are easy to store and ship. Clothes are one of the easiest items to store because they do not need any special equipment or packing requirements. I usually hang items that are high priced and fold those that are not. They do not take up much space too. The same comfort goes when I

ship them, I can fit them on a standard sized parcel and the weight will make it eligible for fixed rate parcels.

3. There is always profit. You cannot simply go wrong with reselling these items, unless you really make bad and obvious decisions in purchasing them. One thing I like is that I can buy them at an even bigger discount if they are damaged such as tears or missing buttons but these are easily repaired which gives me a wider profit margin.

4. You can get a following. Chances are if you are able to sell one item to a satisfied customer, he will be back for more. The target customers of these items are always in the lookout for these items and if you get him a good item for a good price, he will be back. Once you build a relationship with your customer base, you can maintain and even grow it in word of mouth alone.

5. It is a perfect training ground. If you are a beginner, reselling this type of merchandise is a good way to learn the business in preparation for something bigger. Although no business is perfectly risk-free, this business has fewer risks compared to others.

Step Two: Understand Your Merchandise

Anatomy of Blazers, Coats & Suits

Blazers, coats and suits are sometimes used interchangeably. However, as a business owner, it is important for you to know the difference between the three and understand your merchandise. Not only will this help you when you are sourcing your inventory but also give your credibility when you are posting your listing or communicating with your customers.

Blazers are jackets that are made without a matching pair of trousers or pants. It is the most versatile because it can be dressed down with jeans or up with slacks for a more formal look. It can be single or double breasted, with the latter more suited for dressing up.

Sport coats are originally worn by gentlemen and aristocrats hunting in their estates. This is why their designs are mostly done in tweed and in heavier materials. Sport coats have more rustic color palettes and textures. While they also do not have paired trousers like the blazers, they have pockets with flaps.

Lastly, suits are formal fashion pieces. It is always created with a matching pair of trousers. They have a variety of cuts and can be worn with a vest and shirt underneath. They are mostly worn with ties or bowties.

Lapels are the folded collars; they are folded back in the front of jacket. They can either be notch lapels, which are angled downward or peak, which has a fold angled upward. Another kind of lapel, the shawl lapel is gaining popularity as a simple but elegant alternative to the first two kinds of lapels.

These items will have pockets; there are usually two main pockets on either side of the bottom part of the clothing. A patch pocket in the upper left side, which is used to show a folded piece of cloth that matches the shirt underneath. Most will also have inner pockets. Sleeves can have anywhere from two to four buttons on each cuff. Take note that these side buttons cannot be undone. Some of them will have vents, a short slit in the bottom back side of the item, originally intended for ease in horseback riding.

How to Measure Your Merchandise

Proper description is necessary in listing your items for sale and key information needed are the sizes and measurement. While this information can sometimes be found in the item itself, such as the inside labels, some clothes may not have this information and you have to do the measurement yourself. Note that most measurements are taken in inches.

Using a measuring tape, here are some of the areas that you need to measure:

Chest- measure from underneath the left all the way to right armpit
Arms- measure from the armpit to the cuff
Height- measure from the collar in the back to the hem

Take note that the chest size is also the size of the blazer, coat or suit. For example, if your client says that he is a size 40, then you need to check your merchandise for an item with a chest size of also 40.

50 Profitable Brands to Buy & Sell on eBay

While size and materials are two considerations made by your customers, perhaps it is the brands of your items that will motivate them to make the purchase. Consumers today are as conscious with size and materials as with the brand of clothing. The more recognized the brand, the higher the chances of making the sale.

There are several American, European and other global brands that can give you an indication of a sell-able item. The list below is of brands known for their quality, craftsmanship and of their recognition in the blazers, coats and suits industry. Be on the lookout for these brands on your next run in the thrift stores:

1. Anthony Squires
2. Antony Morato
3. Armani
4. Banana Republic
5. BOSS
6. Bottega Veneta
7. Brioni
8. Brunello Cucinelli
9. Burberry
10. Calvin Klein
11. Canali
12. Coppley
13. Corneliani
14. DKNY
15. Dolce & Gabbana
16. Ermenegildo Zegna
17. Etro
18. Fendi
19. Gazman
20. Gieves & Hawkes
21. Giorgio Armani
22. Givenchy
23. Gucci
24. Hardy Amies
25. Hickey Freeman
26. Hugo Boss
27. IZOD
28. Jack Victor
29. J. Lindeberg
30. Joe Black
31. Kenneth Cole
32. Kiton

33. Lanvin
34. Marks & Spencer
35. Moncier
36. Paul Smith
37. Paul Zileri
38. Polo
39. Prada
40. Pronto Uomo
41. Ralph Lauren
42. Ravazzollo
43. Stefano Ricci
44. Tommy Hilfiger
45. Valentino
46. Versace
47. Yves Saint Laurent
48. Z. Zegna
49. Zara
50. Zilli

Also, avoid buying thrifted items that are made in countries in Asia or other developing countries. While they may be able to compete in terms of quality and craftsmanship as with their Western counterparts, buyers usually associate higher levels of quality for items made in European countries.

Customer Profile

It is also important to know who your target customer is. If you are able to determine the demographic, you can have easier and better thrift runs. This is because you know exactly what you are looking for because you have a target customer in mind.

For example, you target customer can be young professionals, who are aware of the brands but are still unable to afford brand new or custom made pieces. When you have this target, you know that this demographic is more fashion forward. They are aware of the trends and not afraid to experiment with colors, cuts or textures.

When you go to your next thrift run and you are unable to decide whether to purchase a particular piece, then you can always refer to your demographic. Will your target, with his style, preference and budget, buy this?

Step Three: Open Your Shop

eBay & Etsy

eBay is one of the best and if not the best online platform for your virtual store. The seller account control panel is very easy to use and it has starter accounts that you can access for free. The reach of eBay is vast and it is a household name for finding clothing similar to your merchandise. One of the features of eBay that make it distinct to other selling platforms is its auction style of selling. Instead of a fixed price, you can set a minimum amount as starting bid and then depending on the demand of your item, you can see the bidding go up more than 10 times its starting bid.

To register as a seller, go to this <u>link</u>.

Etsy is fast becoming an alternative to eBay for vintage clothing. While it was known as a platform for handcrafted items, it is now also carrying fashion items, including blazers, coats and suits. Vintage items have always been synonymous with Etsy and this association makes it a viable option for your reselling business. Although it still does not have the same reach as eBay, this platform can be a potential secondary store for your business. One feature of Etsy is that it allows you to personalize your virtual store, complete with signage, design and color scheme.

To register as a seller, go to this <u>link</u>.

Inventory & Stocking Considerations

One of the biggest mistakes that some startup business owner makes is starting big. The beauty in selling these items or selling online is that you can scale your business as needed. Traditional brick and mortar stores will require you to be fully stocked so you can maximize the space of the store. However, this means a huge investment to create a huge inventory. The risk is that the longer these items stay in the store, the longer is the turnaround of the money.

If you are a beginner in selling these items, start small or with something manageable. eBay lets you start with 20 free listing per month. Use that as your maximum starter inventory. This way, you do not have to incur additional expenses for excess listings but you still get a feel of the selling these items.

Now that you know how many you can sell in the first days of your business, the next step is to know what kind of blazers, coats or suits will make up your starting inventory. A lot of the stocking considerations will depend on:

Passion and expertise
Season
Trend

While your business must be profit driven, it must also be run by your passion and expertise. If blazers are more appealing to you, then you can stock up on a majority of these items first before anything else. Usually blazers are a best starter because of their versatility compare to the more focused clientele of coats or suits.

It is also best to be mindful of the season when you plan to open shop. If you already have an inventory of blazers made of heavy or thick materials, then it may be best to sell them a month or a few weeks before the winter season. This way demand for your items will be higher compared to other months of the year.

Never underestimate the power of trends in the purchasing choices of your customers. For example, during the writing of this book, navy blue blazers, coats and suits are all the rage in the red carpet. This color can be found being worn by celebrities everywhere and for sure there will be a huge demand for items with this color.

When you get your business going and profits, which only started as a trickle, start to flow, it is now time to expand your inventory to larger volumes. Scale up when your eBay account when you get several good finds on your thrift store runs. You can establish yourself as a seller of a wide range of blazers, coats and suits but focusing only on these items as your expertise. You can become a go-to seller in your chosen virtual platform.

Choosing a Business Model to Price & Sell Your Items

There are a variety of business models that you can choose from to help you make a decision in pricing and ultimately selling your items. A business model is a summary of the business processes involved from the choice all the way to the sale of the merchandise.

Some business models that you can choose from are:

Brick and mortar store- this is when you sell your merchandise in a physical store. You need to consider overhead expenses, such as rent, utilities and taxes when pricing your items or when targeting your profit margins. You can store and sell your items in larger quantities because of the space that is in your disposal.

Virtual store- this is when you use eBay or Etsy as your virtual store. You can certainly cut back on expenses but you need to devote time in listing your items and setting up your payment channels. You also need to build your reputation before you can get any credibility in the online business. You can price your items low and the reach of your items are almost worldwide, if you make your merchandise easily searchable.

Distribution- instead of selling direct to consumers, you can do it via middlemen. You can let them do the work for you but they will receive a portion of the profits. This model works when you have extremely large quantities of merchandise that you need to move but you do not have time to attend to them one by one.

Fixed vs. Auction- if you will use eBay as one of your stores you can choose between a fixed and an auction style business model. In fixed price, you can set one price for your customers to buy the item. If you have an auction, you can set it at a low price, usually at least the same amount as your original buying prices and let the customers determine how much they want to buy it. You can also make it a combination between the two, set your eBay listing so that you there is a starting bid and a buy now option for determined buyers.

Loyalty programs- you can augment your business by providing loyal clientele with certain perks and benefits. You can offer a discount on the second item purchased or a first pick option for your new items. Whatever their choice is, it will be a guaranteed sale for you.

Your shipping cost will also be an important factor in pricing your items. Fortunately, blazers, coats and suits are very lightweight and not breakable, which means you do not need special packing materials and you will not incur any additional shipping charges. You may ask why shipping account for the price when you can easily have your customer shoulder the shipping charges.

Some business owners make the mistake of charging their customers with the cost of the shipping not knowing that shouldering the cost by offering free shipping is quite profitable and beneficial. Firstly, no customer can resist a seller that offer free shipping. It gives them the illusion that they are really getting it for free or that the item cost is high because the shipping fee is already included in it. This means your customers are already justifying to themselves the cost of the item, which may lead them to actually purchasing the item in the end.

Offering free shipping can also be profitable. For example, your intended selling price is at $5 and you add $3 for shipping. When you get the total cost for the shipping, you find out that it will only cost you $2. This means you have an extra dollar on top of the profit when you priced it at $5.

6 Profitable Selling Points & Other Tips to Boost Sales

As profitable as these items are, they will not sell themselves. You need to be able to highlight their key selling points to make the deal. Here are 6 points that you can emphasize to convince your potential clients to purchase your merchandise.

The brand- no other selling point can beat the brand. If you have an item that belongs to any of the high or middle end brands in the market, then you definitely need to highlight it. Your customers will most probably be aware of the brand in the first place and if not, he will do his research on it. Consider putting the brand in the title and add a picture of the label in the listing.

Take note though, you have to be sure that what you have is authentic. There are several knock offs of these items, especially branded ones. Do your research in determining authenticity or have it verified by an appraiser. If you are selling in eBay, saying that an item is authentic but when the customer finds out that it is not, is grounds for a return or refund.

The trend- another selling point is to associate your item with the current fashion trend when you made it available on your store. When your item is similar to the ones being worn by celebrities and other personalities, it will add that much needed motivation to make the purchase.

The rarity- if you can genuinely establish that your item is truly one of a kind or only few left in existence, then it adds a whole new level of desirability for it. Nothing incites a customer to purchase something if he knows that either he will be the only one who will have it or only few others will have the same item.

The progeny- your customers love a good story and they will love it even more if they can be a part of the story itself. If you can establish that your item was part of the estate of a disgraced old moneyed aristocrat in the Hamptons, then the story can create a highly desirable progeny that no customer will be able to resist

The potential- these items are very versatile but sometimes your customers will not be able to see their potential by themselves. Mention that it can be used at work, at the party, for informal or formal occasions. Show your customers that even if they are buying only one item, its many uses and functions make it appropriate for more than one event.

The promise- you can establish yourself as a true connoisseur of blazers, sports coats and suits. Add a clause that says that returning customers are given first or priority pick of your next batch of finds. This gives your customers not only a sense of importance but also may guarantee repeat business or interest in your store.

If you will notice, I did not include quality of material, condition and the price of the items. While these are good selling points, they do not belong to my top 6 selling points. Why? Blazers, sports coats and suits, as well as other fashion items, are not really purchases made out of reason or logic but out of emotion and preference. Sale of these items rely more on the appeal they can make to your target customers.

For example, if you have two blazers that are made of the same material, in the same condition and in the same price but one was bought from an Upper East Side sale while the other from an unknown store in the outskirts of town, then the customer will most probably choose the Upper East Side blazer. It gives them the feeling that in one way or another, they are associated with the place.

Price or more specifically low prices are also highly discouraged as selling points. Studies show that consumers today associate high prices with better quality and low prices with poorer quality. The lower you price your items or when you highlight how cheap your items are, your consumers may associate the price with the lack of quality. Avoid using words like cheap, second hand or used.

Finally, be honest. It may seem counterintuitive to highlight imperfection, such as a tear, a scratch or a stain but your customers will appreciate it. They will know that you are transparent and you are determined to have the best customer experience for them. Make sure to mention them in your listing.

How to Take Fantastic Pictures

While you can always hire an expert photographer to take pictures of your merchandise for your listing, this will only add up as an expense and reduce your profit. You do not have to be an expert photographer to take fantastic pictures but you have to make good decisions. There are three major considerations that you need to make when taking pictures:

Artistic
Technical
Informational

I usually stage my items before I take a picture of them. Staging borrows from the technique used by real estate agents in selling homes. Instead of selling a bare house, they deck it with complete furniture, turn on the lights and show buyers the potential of the house. You can do the same for your items.

Instead of hanging your item by itself, you have several options to stage your merchandise. First you can invest on a mannequin, the upper body will do but if you have the budget you can opt for a full body mannequin. Pair a navy blue jacket with a white striped shirt and basic jeans for a casual look or with a vest and tie and black pants for a more formal look. Show any accessories that match the blazer, like shoes, belts or bags. Although you are only selling the blazer itself, your picture will show your customers the potential of the blazer. For an even better picture, make a collage of all potential combinations that the blazer can be paired with for different occasions. If you are or if you have a friend with a perfect body to model the blazer, you can also take pictures of the blazer in a live setting.

Of course, before taking the pictures, make sure you clean and iron your items. Cut any loose threads and use a lint remover if needed. Spot cleaners will be one of your most important tools for taking the best picture. Another item you need is clothespins. Pin any excess fabric or slack to make the perfect fit for your mannequin or model to show the best possible image of your item.

When you take pictures, whether you hang your items, put in a mannequin or have it worn by a model, make sure you take pictures from all angles. Front, side, back, zoomed in and out are some of the usual angles that you can consider. You can also take pictures of the lining of the items. Take a picture of any hardware, such as buttons or cufflinks.

Take pictures in a room with bright and natural light. While a camera flash can provide the lighting you need, it sometimes distorts the texture of the material and changes the color of the item.

Take pictures of any feature that you want to highlight, such as the brand, material or pattern. Also, if there are imperfections or damages, make sure to take a picture of those too. When you list down small stain on left sleeve, make sure to take a picture of that stain. This will give your customers a visual indication of the extent of the damage.

Never take a photo of your items when they are folded on the floor or on your bed. It will take away the angles that can give you the sale. Also, due to copyright issues, you cannot copy and paste a picture of the item from a website, catalogue or any other source aside from your own. eBay will remove your listing if you do this. Plus, your customers will immediately feel doubtful of not only your item but your entire merchandise if you only show pictures of brand new items instead of the actual merchandise itself.

How to Create an Amazing eBay Listing

Your pictures play a major part in convincing your customers to make the purchase but it will be your listing that will lead them to the final decision. While the picture will take care of the emotional appeal of your item, your listing is responsible for the logical reasoning that will convince your customers to make the purchase. Your listing will let them know the fine print that can motivate them to buy your item. Here are three important considerations to create an amazing eBay listing:

Title- for search-ability
Information- for transparency
Lingo- for credibility

The first thing that your customers will read after looking at the picture is the title. Remember, your customers use search words to find what they need in eBay. This means you need to put yourself in the shoes of your customers. What words will they most likely use when they are looking for your merchandise? The usual words they will use, along with the actual blazer, sports coat or suit, will be color and brand. For example, a typical search for a suit will be black, double breasted, Hugo Boss blazer. Whatever keywords are used, those must be in the title.

Now you can list the facts and figures of the item. You need to include all dimensions, such as sizes, material and most importantly condition. Add the brand and the profile of the manufacturer. Include any other information that your customer may want to know in not only buying your item but also something that is used.

Do not be afraid to use eBay lingo, most of your customers will be returning clients to eBay and they will most probably be familiar with the lingo. This gives you the credibility of being a long time seller in eBay. Some of the related eBay lingo that you can use that is appropriate for selling your items:

OOAK- one of a kind
NWT- new with tags
HTF- hard to find
Pre-loved- better way to say used or second hand

How to Break Down Your Profits

When the money flows in to your accounts, you need to set aside time to study your financials. The more you understand your cash flow, the better decisions you can make for your business. Blazers, coats and suits may be your expertise and buying and selling thrifted items may be your passion but without a solid financial foundation to build on, your business is in danger of crumbling down. You need to break down your profits to fully understand the financial side of your business.

First, you need to make the distinction between revenue and profit. Revenue is your total amount of sales for a given month or year. For planning purposes, it is best to compute in a per month basis. Monthly budgeting will give you an idea of the trends of sales and at the same time coincide with some of the expenses that are being charged to your business, like subscription fees.

On the other hand, revenue less expenses is equal to your profit. Whatever remains from your revenue, after all appropriate expenses have been charged to it, can already be considered your profit.

Here are some potential expense items for your business

1. Monthly subscription fees- these are any recurring fees charged for memberships or upgrades to your virtual accounts
2. Commission fees of your virtual stores- for example eBay charges you a 10% fee
3. Promotional materials and supplies- mannequins, hangers or ads
4. Storage, packing and shipping supplies- tape, bubble wrap, Ziploc etc.
5. Gas and travel expenses for thrifting and restocking

Now that you have your expenses listed down, it is now time to breakdown your profits. Some of the funds that can be filled up by your profit are:

1. New inventory- as you increase your profits, you must scale up your fund for restocking your inventory. This way your business grows along with your profit.
2. Investment- set aside a certain percentage or amount of your profits towards investment. It can either be used as a fund to expand your business for a different set of merchandise or to fund an entirely new business venture.
3. Savings- this is a fund that can be used as a buffer for lean months. Dip into this fund to pay for any deferred payment that is meant to be paid as expense during regular business operations.

Packing Your Items to be Shipped

Your merchandise requires no special container to ship. However, it pays to be extra careful in shipping your items so that your clients will receive the item intact and without damage. Neatly fold the purchased items, you can either use your bare hands or use a folding guide for the perfect fold.

Next seal it first with thin sheet of paper or even a zip lock bag. Tissue paper will be enough but if you are expecting bad weather, it is best for your items to be shipped in waterproof container. Then before you seal it, add loose paper or packing paper to create a cushion. Tape it firmly and make sure to cover any crack or opening. Also, if you are eBay buyer yourself, you can recycle old boxes and containers sent to you as a way to reduce cost and also be environmentally responsible.

Although not necessary, you can add a thank you or personal note to your customer. Make sure it is short and handwritten. It will add that personal touch that will definitely increase the chances for a return in business.

Be very prompt in shipment, as soon as payment is cleared, your customers expect shipment in at most a day. If one day is too short for you, then inform them of your handling time in your listing. A handling time gives your customers an idea of how long it will take you to ship items upon their payment. Send them the shipping details as soon as you can. If there are issues that may cause delay, be transparent. It is best to inform your customers as soon as the issues arise before they find it out on their own.

Most Effective Shipping Method

USPS is the most cost effective shipping method for your merchandise. It is very convenient and you can access the First Class option since your items are below 13 oz. If you can print shipping labels, then you can simply drop off the item in a post box instead of lining up in the post office. Make sure to fold your shipment in such a way that it will fit the post box slot.

The USPS First Class will ship your items in less than 5 days. For Priority Mail, it will be shipped in less than 3 days. Express can be delivered in less than 2 days. Your virtual store can be accessed worldwide. In case you require international or faster, shipment, you can use DHL, FedEx or UPS for your shipping needs.

5 Things to Consider to Reducing Your eBay Price

In a perfect world, all your merchandise will sell at the price that you want. However, not everything will go your way in life or in business. You may have to consider reducing your price to make the sale. Here are some things to consider for price reductions:

1. How will the reduction affect the bottom line? Make sure that the price reduction will not result to a loss. Breaking even is a last resort for price reduction.
2. Can you sell it a later time? Timing, such as season or trend, is always a factor for your merchandise. If you have enough storage space or other items to sell, then you can opt to postpone reduction of the price and wait for the demand to increase.
3. How does it fare against similar items? Do a quick research on similar items, compare your item and the price you set for it. If it is way above the market prices, then you may

consider reducing it but if it is about the same or even lower, then you may hold on to the price.

4. Can you sell it as an add-on? If you are already in the cross and up sell stage, then you may be able to avoid reduction if you sell the item as part of a set.

5. When you have done all considerations and the result is still to reduce the price, then make the change. However, use it as a lesson for you. Record the circumstances that necessitated the price reduction and apply your learning on your future business decisions.

Step Four: Cross & Up Sell

When your business has taken off the best next step to do is to expand. This can be done by either cross or up selling. Cross selling means that you offer your clientele merchandise that can be bought together with your main inventory. In this case, you can cross sell items that can be worn or paired with jackets, coats or suits.

On the other hand, up selling means you offer items that are similar to those that you are currently selling but are of higher quality and of course at a higher price. These are premium items that you can sell based on your reputation or through your long relationship with your clients.

Some of the items that you can add on top your main merchandise are:

1. Shirts &Vests- these are items that worn underneath your main merchandise. When you open your store for shirts, you will be inundated with several options in thrift stores. As a starter, choose solid colors first before venturing out to more adventurous prints. Also, make it a point to match your shirts and vests with blazers, coats and suits that you already have in stock.
2. Ties, Belts &Cufflinks- these may not be as lucractive as with the rest of your merchandise but their purpose is for staging your main merchandise. This way you can add up a certain amount so that ties can be sold as a set.
3. Scarves & Gloves- these are very seasonal but when you have them in store at the right time, you can be sure to reap in the profits. Take note to stock up on these items several weeks or a couple of months prior to the colder seasons so that your store is ready for the demand.
4. Shoes- these are another source of big profits, especially when you chance upon branded and high quality leather items. However, these are notoriously fleeting because of the fast paced changing of the trends. Be on the lookout for trends, especially since the older styles

such as oxfors and brogues are in fashion during the
writing of this book.

5. Hats- although these items were once only considered
   seasonal or for more mature clientele, hats are making
   a comeback even for younger customers. Make sure to
   keep these items in your inventory.

While cross or up selling are certainly lucrative, do not be
tempted to do it immediately or when you are just starting in
the business. The danger in doing it prematurely is that you
lose focus of your primary merchandise, which should be
blazers, coats and suits. You may end up spending more than
you should on your next thrifting run or you will have too
much cross or up sell merchandise than your main
merchandise. Remember, in eBay you only have 20 free
listings and every additional one for your cross or up sell
merchandise will require a listing of their own, which is an
additional expense.

The best time to cross or up sell is when you already have a
significant amount of traffic or a set of loyal clients, who
regularly visit or purchase from you. Of course, as the business
owner, the decision is still entirely yours on the timing of this
next business activity.

Step Five: Build a Network

One of the many advantages of the online reselling business is that you can virtually run the business on your own, saving you hundreds of dollars from overhead expenses such as wages or salary. On the other hand, this does not mean that you can be self-reliant at all times.

In this business of reselling blazers, coats and suits, you need to build a network of professionals, which can help you become more profitable in your business. The cost of their services will certainly be well justified by the improvement on your merchandise, pricing scheme or other facets of the business.

Tailors

Your DIY repair skills will certainly reach its limit when you encounter thrifted items that are too good to pass but are too damaged to turn in for a profit. In these situations, it is best to have a partnership with a tailor, who can do the repairs for you. Aside from repairs, the tailor can also resize the items that are too large to fit your usual clientele. Tailors can replace linings, hardware; create pockets and any other tweaks that you may request. A trusted tailor is truly invaluable in this business as they can mean the difference between a loss and a profit.

Appraisers

One of the best rewards of thrifting is that you can come across a piece of clothing that is valuable, rare or already one of a kind. The problem is that you may not be aware of it. One of the most common mistakes that owners of this type of business make is to either over or under price an item. Appraisers are your best bet when you come across a blazer, coat or suit that you are unfamiliar with or are unconfident in pricing.

Other Sellers

It may seem counterintuitive for you to build a network with your competition but it does have its benefits. When you become a part of the reselling community, you essentially gain access to their clientele. If you distinguish yourself with your merchandise, one seller may refer his client to you if you have something that the other seller does not have. While commissions or finder's fee are certainly part of the deal, a sale is still a sale.

Another advantage is that you can join them on their thrifting runs. While you may know all of the thrift stores in town, you may not be fully aware of a closed estate sale, a newly opened auction or other sources of potential merchandise.

Appendix 1: Quick Action Guide & Checklist

Here is a Quick Action with a Checklist to help you get started and get organized on your reselling business:

Action 1: Know the Market
Checklist

Familiarize yourself on your merchandise
Make a quick research on current prices
Current trends and seasonal needs

Action 2: Source your Inventory
Checklist:

Current inventory
Money, time and other resources
Network of thrift stores
List of profitable brands
Network of partners and professionals

Action 3: Open your Business
Checklist

eBay or Etsy account
Linked Paypal account
Camera and other staging requirements
Measurements, information and other content for your listing

Action 4: Run your Business
Checklist

Monthly cash flow, including revenue, expenses and profit
Shipping supplies and partners
Promotions, such as social media

Action 5: Care for your Merchandise
Checklist

Threads, pins and other repair supplies
Hangers, plastic, hanging rods and other organizing supplies
Stain removers, ironing board, steamers etc.

Appendix 2: 50 Examples of Blazers Sold on eBay for a Great Return

1. http://www.ebay.co.uk/itm/NEW-Antony-Morato-Blazer-Navy-SIZE-L-50-RRP-129-00-/161719926298
2. http://www.ebay.com/itm/GIORGIO-ARMANI-Men-Jacket-Blazer-Size-50-/221783541574
3. http://www.ebay.com/itm/BANANA-REPUBLIC-BLACK-100-WOOL-3-BUTTON-BLAZER-JACKET-SPORT-COAT-MENS-42L-/261910040105?pt=LH_DefaultDomain_0&hash=item3cf b0e0e29
4. http://www.ebay.com/itm/Hugo-Boss-Mens-Sport-Coat-Blazer-Jacket-Double-Breast-Striped-Size-42-/261899999528?pt=LH_DefaultDomain_0&hash=item3c fa74d928
5. http://www.ebay.com/itm/MINT-Mens-BRIONI-Recent-Navy-Blue-2-Btn-Augusto-Sports-Coat-Blazer-/261910023627?pt=LH_DefaultDomain_0&hash=item3cf b0dcdcb
6. http://www.ebay.com/itm/BRUNELLO-CUCINELLI-Mens-Navy-White-Micro-Checkered-Three-Button-Wool-Blazer-/141648812458?pt=LH_DefaultDomain_0&hash=item20f aed59aa
7. http://www.ebay.com/itm/BEAUTIFUL-MEN-S-BURBERRY-BLAZER-TLC-SIZE-38S-/151694677063?pt=LH_DefaultDomain_0&hash=item23 51b51447
8. http://www.ebay.com/itm/CALVIN-KLEIN-MENS-48-R-SILK-LINEN-WOOL-WINDOWPANE-PLAID-SPORT-COAT-BLAZER-/351412326132?pt=LH_DefaultDomain_0&hash=item51d 1ce8ef4
9. http://www.ebay.com/itm/Canali-Proposta-Bernini-100-Wool-Mens-Sport-Coat-Jacket-Blazer-Size-54-R-Eu-/261900026998?pt=LH_DefaultDomain_0&hash=item3c fa754476

10. http://www.ebay.com/itm/COPPLEY-mens-gray-wool-blazer-size-43-44-R-/221769536681?pt=LH_DefaultDomain_0&hash=item33a27e94a9

11. http://www.ebay.com/itm/Corneliani-Mens-40R-Brown-Window-Pane-Wool-Cashmere-Blazer-Sportscoat-Italy-3-B-/231556091434?pt=LH_DefaultDomain_0&hash=item35e9d18e2a

12. http://www.ebay.com/itm/DKNY-Donna-Karan-Signature-Mens-Black-Italian-Wool-Blazer-Sportcoat-44-R-WOW-/271880305557?pt=LH_DefaultDomain_0&hash=item3f4d543b95

13. http://www.ebay.com/itm/Mens-Dolce-Gabbana-Dark-Gray-Plaid-Wool-Blend-Two-Button-Blazer-Jacket-52-/391139584405?pt=LH_DefaultDomain_0&hash=item5b11bc6995

14. http://www.ebay.com/itm/ENGLISH-LAUNDRY-Mens-EVERLONG-BLAZER-striped-silver-black-JACKET-Medium-/121644159960?pt=LH_DefaultDomain_2&hash=item1c528e93d8

15. http://www.ebay.com/itm/Mens-Ermenegildo-Zegna-Blazer-Jacket-40R-40-R-SOFT-Black-Tan-Check-3-button-/221788791466?pt=LH_DefaultDomain_0&hash=item33a3a462aa

16. http://www.ebay.com/itm/Mens-ETRO-Navy-Blue-Cotton-Summer-Blazer-Jacket-54L-/271883122060?hash=item3f4d7f358c

17. http://www.ebay.com/itm/Fendi-Mens-Grey-3-Button-Blazer-Size-44R-/400925713896?pt=LH_DefaultDomain_0&hash=item5d5908e5e8

18. http://www.ebay.com/itm/GIEVES-HAWKES-SAVILE-ROW-MENS-2-BTN-WOOL-SPORT-COAT-BLAZER-JACKET-40R-40-REG-

/291198158582?pt=LH_DefaultDomain_0&hash=item43c
cc346f6

19. http://www.ebay.com/itm/Mens-Giorgio-Armani-Le-
Collezioni-Double-Breasted-Olive-Green-Blazer-Jacket-
/311369390576?pt=LH_DefaultDomain_0&hash=item48
7f0fd9f0

20. http://www.ebay.com/itm/40R-Givenchy-Mens-Navy-
Blue-100-Wool-CLASSIC-FIT-Sport-Coat-Blazer-Jacket-
/381267236654?pt=LH_DefaultDomain_0&hash=item58
c54c572e

21. http://www.ebay.com/itm/Gucci-mens-gray-wool-blazer-
jacket-coat-46-US36-chest-1900-
/261884470006?pt=LH_DefaultDomain_0&hash=item3c
f987e2f6

22. http://www.ebay.com/itm/HARDY-AMIES-MENS-
CLASSIC-CAMEL-TAN-WOOL-BLAZER-SIZE-42-REG-
/221769236294?pt=LH_DefaultDomain_0&hash=item33
a279ff46

23. http://www.ebay.com/itm/HICKEY-FREEMAN-
BESPOKE-MENS-SZ-40-R-TAN-2-BTN-SPORT-COAT-
BLAZER-JACKET-JWC-
/400924700684?pt=LH_DefaultDomain_0&hash=item5
d58f9700c

24. http://www.ebay.com/itm/Boss-Hugo-Boss-Mens-
Pinstripe-Blazer-
/261903232014?pt=LH_DefaultDomain_0&hash=item3cf
aa62c0e

25. http://www.ebay.com/itm/Mens-IZOD-Navy-Wool-2-
Button-Blazer-W-Elbow-Patches-44R-EUC-98-
/251897807574?pt=LH_DefaultDomain_0&hash=item3a
a64782d6

26. http://www.ebay.com/itm/mens-gray-JACK-VICTOR-
blazer-jacket-loretowood-sport-coat-bamboo-soft-42-L-
/181760427385?pt=LH_DefaultDomain_0&hash=item2a
51c40579

27. http://www.ebay.com/itm/MENS-J-LINDEBERG-
STOCKHOLM-TWEED-STRIPED-SPORT-COAT-
BLAZER-SIZE-40-EURO-50-

/291480354576?pt=LH_DefaultDomain_0&hash=item43
dd953f10

28. http://www.ebay.com/itm/Mens-Joe-Namath-Black-Gray-Sports-Jacket-Coat-Blazer-48-/151653913294?pt=LH_DefaultDomain_0&hash=item234
f4712ce

29. http://www.ebay.com/itm/Kenneth-Cole-Reaction-Mens-Blazer-43-Regular-100-Wool-Suit-Coat-Jacket-43R-/361286474322?pt=LH_DefaultDomain_0&hash=item54
1e5a1a52

30. http://www.ebay.com/itm/KITON-Mens-Navy-Three-Button-Wool-Blazer-BEAUTIFUL-/131495740493?pt=LH_DefaultDomain_0&hash=item1e9
dc1c44d

31. http://www.ebay.com/itm/Lanvin-Paris-Wool-Blazer-Sport-Coat-Jacket-Mens-Gold-Buttons-46R-VTG-Tan-CLEAN-/281708049548?pt=LH_DefaultDomain_0&hash=item41
971bb48c

32. http://www.ebay.com/itm/Mens-Marks-Spencer-Tweed-Jacket-Blazer-46S-AR6990-/131505849155?pt=LH_DefaultDomain_3&hash=item1e9
e5c0343

33. http://www.ebay.com/itm/Paul-Smith-Mens-Black-Three-Button-100-Wool-Blazer-38-/371333271986?pt=LH_DefaultDomain_0&hash=item567
53011b2

34. http://www.ebay.com/itm/Paul-Zileri-Gruppo-Forall-Mens-Brown-Herringbone-Blazer-Sport-Coat-Size-44L-/261880287326?pt=LH_DefaultDomain_0&hash=item3c
f948105e

35. http://www.ebay.com/itm/Mens-POLO-Cream-Colored-Linen-Sports-Coat-Blazer-Jacket-Size-Medium-/221782215049?pt=LH_DefaultDomain_0&hash=item33
a3400989

36. http://www.ebay.com/itm/Prada-MENS-Black-2-Button-jacket-BLAZER-52-Euro-42-US-/201360669323?pt=LH_DefaultDomain_0&hash=item2e
e207fa8b

37. http://www.ebay.com/itm/PRONTO-UOMO-MENS-BLAZER-40S-SUPER-120-FRABIC-100-WOOL-BLACK-PIN-STRIP-/291475309783?pt=LH_DefaultDomain_0&hash=item43dd4844d7

38. http://www.ebay.com/itm/Mens-Lauren-Ralph-Lauren-Blazer-Sport-Coat-Green-Plaid-Size-50L-/151698308621?pt=LH_DefaultDomain_0&hash=item2351ec7e0d

39. http://www.ebay.com/itm/Ravazzolo-Mens-Blue-Sports-Jacket-Blazer-Italy-Hand-Tailored-SZ-48-38-/201359593054?pt=LH_DefaultDomain_0&hash=item2ee1f78e5e

40. http://www.ebay.com/itm/NEW-Stunning-STEFANO-RICCI-Recent-Denim-Cotton-3-Btn-Blue-Blazer-Sz-40-R-/231573601751?pt=LH_DefaultDomain_0&hash=item35eadcbdd7

41. http://www.ebay.com/itm/Tommy-Hilfiger-Blazer-Men-Sport-Coat-Jacket-Size-44R-Suits-Tan-Beige-/201362181355?pt=LH_DefaultDomain_0&hash=item2ee21f0ceb

42. http://www.ebay.com/itm/Mens-Silk-N-Valentino-Blazer-/161715748162?pt=LH_DefaultDomain_0&hash=item25a7027d42

43. http://www.ebay.com/itm/Yves-Saint-Laurent-mens-blazer-Brown-Size-40-Made-in-France-/251978490175?pt=LH_DefaultDomain_0&hash=item3aab16a13f

44. http://www.ebay.com/itm/Ermenegildo-Zegna-Z-Zegna-100-White-Linen-Lightweight-Blazer-Coat-SZ-56-46-L-/221782208203?pt=LH_DefaultDomain_0&hash=item33a33feecb

45. http://www.ebay.com/itm/ZARA-Man-Black-2-Button-Blazer-Sport-Coat-Pocket-36-USA-46-EURO-Cotton-/391144560429?pt=LH_DefaultDomain_0&hash=item5b1208572d

46. http://www.ebay.com/itm/198-Calvin-Klein-Mens-Black-Corduroy-Blazer-Size-Small-S-Authentic-One-Button-

/181744735508?pt=LH_DefaultDomain_0&hash=item2a50d49514

47. http://www.ebay.com/itm/Gucci-Italy-Silk-Blend-2-Button-Silver-Vented-Blazer-Mens-40L-MSRP-1875-00-/151669621542?pt=LH_DefaultDomain_0&hash=item235036c326

48. http://www.ebay.com/itm/Balenciaga-Charcoal-black-men-jacket-blazer-domas-style-50-/121664105554?pt=LH_DefaultDomain_0&hash=item1c53beec52

49. http://www.ebay.com/itm/GIORGIO-ARMANI-Le-Collezioni-Wool-Navy-Blue-3-Button-Suit-Blazer-Coat-Mens-39-R-/181756787631?pt=LH_DefaultDomain_0&hash=item2a518c7baf

50. http://www.ebay.com/itm/Prada-Milano-Brown-Sportcoat-50R-It-40R-US-Made-In-Italy/271874404192?_trksid=p2047675.c100005.m1851&_trkparms=aid%3D222007%26algo%3DSIC.MBE%26ao%3D1%26asc%3D20131003132420%26meid%3D564c1fd662be4fb6a7acffde4b7265c6%26pid%3D100005%26rk%3D3%26rkt%3D6%26sd%3D181756787631&rt=nc

Conclusion

The reselling business is relatively safe but exciting, easy but profitable and small but quick to grow business. Now that you are fully equipped with the basic information on the business, you can jumpstart your venture with confidence. In the economy today, having an additional source of income is becoming more and more necessary.

Remember, even if you have all the information you need to start and run the business, without the passion for this kind of endeavor, your venture may fail. If hunting for that great deal in the thrift store, getting the thrill of the sale and negotiating with suppliers and customers alike are your interest; this business is definitely for you.

Also, blazers, coats and suits are only one facet of the reselling industry. Soon enough, with passion and proper business choices, you can venture out to other merchandise, you can cross and up sell and gain profit from entirely different customer profiles and segments.

Source your blazers, coats and suits at thrift shops today and tomorrow begin to earn your much deserved profits!

Check Out & Profit From My Other Books

Below you'll find some of my other popular books that are popular on Amazon and Kindle as well. Simply click on the links below to check them out.

How To Make Money Online

http://www.amazon.com/gp/product/B00S6TOJ5Y

The YouTube Manifesto

http://www.amazon.com/gp/product/B00WBVXHLA

Pick It, Flip It & Thrift It

http://www.amazon.com/gp/product/B00T25NSSK

Thriftology 101

http://www.amazon.com/gp/product/B00R3XNVL2

If the links do not work, for whatever reason, you can simply search for these titles on the Amazon website to find them.

www.ingramcontent.com/pod-product-compliance
Lightning Source LLC
Chambersburg PA
CBHW070230210526
45168CB00019B/1413